THE WORLD AROUND US

ON THE INTERNET

Our First Talk About Online Safety

Dr. Jillian Roberts   Illustrations by Jane Heinrichs

ORCA BOOK PUBLISHERS

I dedicate this book to the founding advisors of FamilySparks, who inspired me to help children and families in this new, challenging digital age. Specifically, I would like to thank Brent Sternig, Andrew Wooldridge, Owen Matthews, Duncan MacRae, Morgan MacRae, Chris Considine, Harvey Huebsch and Claudia Blum. Special gratitude goes to my co-founders, Rasool Rayani, Hannes Blum and Erin Skillen, and to my FamilySparks teammates, Deanna Ladret and Kate Cluley.
—J.R.

For my husband, the best thing the internet ever sent me.
—J.H.

Text copyright © Jillian Roberts 2019, 2022
Illustrations copyright © Jane Heinrichs 2019, 2022

Published in Canada and the United States in 2022 by Orca Book Publishers.
Previously published in 2019 by Orca Book Publishers as a
hardcover (ISBN 9781459820944) and available as an
ebook (ISBN 9781459820951, PDF; ISBN 9781459820968, EPUB).
orcabook.com

Library and Archives Canada Cataloguing in Publication
Title: On the internet : our first talk about online safety /
Dr. Jillian Roberts ; illustrations by Jane Heinrichs.
Names: Roberts, Jillian, 1971- author. | Heinrichs, Jane, 1982- illustrator.
Series: World around us (Orca Book Publishers)
Description: Series statement: The world around us | Previously published:
Victoria, British Columbia : Orca Book Publishers, 2019.
Identifiers: Canadiana 20210248696 | ISBN 9781459833661 (softcover)
Subjects: LCSH: Internet and children—Juvenile literature. |
LCSH: Internet—Safety measures—Juvenile literature.
Classification: LCC HQ784.I58 R53 2022 | DDC j004.67/8083—dc23

Library of Congress Control Number: 2021941326

Summary: Using illustrations, full-color photographs and straightforward text,
this nonfiction picture book introduces the topic of online safety.

Orca Book Publishers is committed to reducing the consumption of
nonrenewable resources in the production of our books. We make
every effort to use materials that support a sustainable future.

Orca Book Publishers gratefully acknowledges the support for its publishing programs
provided by the following agencies: the Government of Canada,
the Canada Council for the Arts and the Province of British Columbia
through the BC Arts Council and the Book Publishing Tax Credit.

Artwork created using English watercolors and
Japanese brush pens on Italian watercolor paper.

Cover and interior art by Jane Heinrichs
Edited by Liz Kemp
Design by Rachel Page

Front cover photos:
iStock.com
Back cover photos (left to right): Shutterstock.com, iStock.com, stocksy.com
Interior photos:
iStock.com: © Portra p. 4, Marilyn Nieves p. 5, kate_sept2004 p. 6,
PeopleImages p. 7, JackF p. 8, globalstock p. 11, Daisy-Daisy p. 12, martin-dm p. 13, svetikd
p. 16, Wavebreakmedia p. 17, Fertnig p. 18, shapecharge p. 19,
PeopleImages p. 20, Steve Debenport p. 22, SolStock p. 23, funstock p. 24,
SolStock p. 25, gradyreese p. 28, PeopleImages p. 29
Stocksy.com: © MaaHoo Studio p. 9, Suprijono Suharjoto p. 10,
aaronbelford inc p. 21, alto images p. 26
Shutterstock.com: © Uber Images p. 14, Iam_Anupong p. 15

Printed and bound in Canada.

25 24 23 22 • 1 2 3 4

○─○

The Internet is full of interesting information.

It's a nice way to communicate with friends or family you don't always get to see in real life. And it's an excellent resource for learning about things that interest you.

But there are things on the Internet that are *not* very good. When you go online at home, at school or with friends, you might see some things you don't understand. Maybe you have clicked on something without being sure what it means or where it will lead.
It's okay to ask questions when you see something you don't understand or if you aren't sure what is safe to look at.

○─○─○─○─○─○─○─   ─○─○─○─○─○─○─○

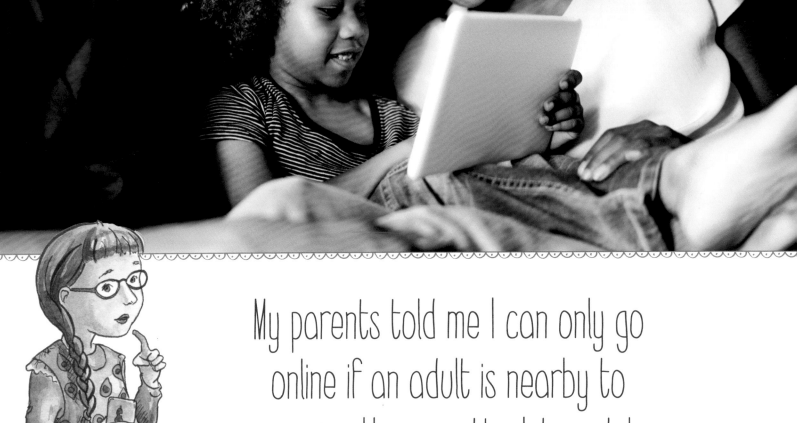

My parents told me I can only go online if an adult is nearby to supervise. How can the Internet be unsafe if it's inside my computer?

People can put anything they want to on the Internet—words, pictures and videos. Most people post things that are interesting or nice to see. But sometimes people use the Internet to say unkind things or behave in ways that are *inappropriate* or mean—just like people do in real life.

There are also some things on the Internet that kids might not understand yet, sort of like how there are books and movies that are just for adults, and others that are for kids. Your parents want to make sure you see only things that are safe and appropriate.

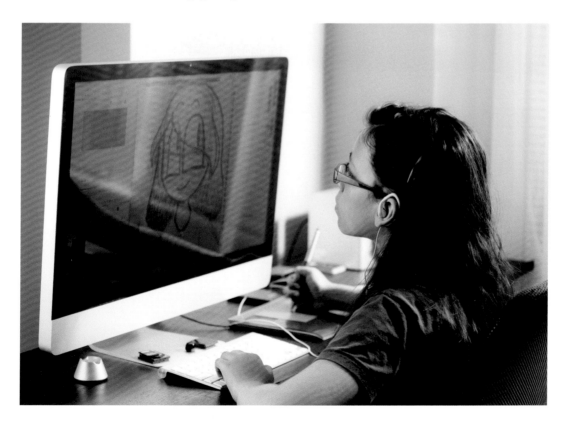

What Does Inappropriate Mean?

Inappropriate means that something is not okay for that purpose or situation. For example, wearing sandals in the snow is an inappropriate choice. Sometimes people talk about or want to show you things that are inappropriate. They might share too many personal details or details about someone else that weren't okay to share.

Parental Controls

Parental controls help block inappropriate, harmful and upsetting content that you can easily stumble upon online. They can also limit in-app purchases and manage the amount of time you spend online. These controls help you keep a healthy relationship with the Internet and your overall use of technology.

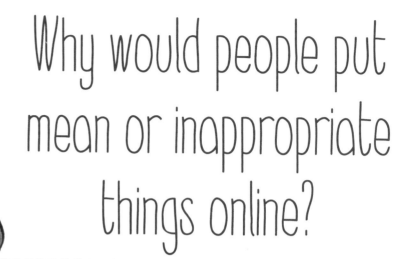

Why would people put mean or inappropriate things online?

What Is Good Judgment?

Good judgment is the ability to think deeply about something and form a wise opinion about it. Deciding what is right and wrong, or good and bad, requires good judgment. However, determining what is right and what is wrong can be very difficult.

What Are Boundaries?

Boundaries are kind of an invisible safety fence. They are the "rules" or limits we create to help us determine safe and appropriate ways for other people to behave toward us. They also help us decide how to respond if someone breaks our rules. It is important to respect boundaries, your own and those of other people.

Sometimes people who feel angry about something decide to share their thoughts on the internet. At other times, people post personal things about themselves or somebody else because they are looking for attention or trying to be funny. People who do this are not exercising *good judgment* or respecting *boundaries*—other people's or their own.

What kinds of boundaries
are there?

One kind of boundary is your "personal bubble," which is the space around your body that belongs to you. It often feels uncomfortable when someone—especially someone you do not know very well—sits or stands too close to you, or talks to you right up close to your face, doesn't it? When someone is doing that, they are crossing a boundary—your personal-space boundary.

How can somebody on the Internet cross a boundary when they are not actually near me?

There are other kinds of boundaries too. When people on the Internet share too much private information about themselves or someone else, the ones who see it often feel really uncomfortable. The people oversharing have crossed another kind of boundary—a *privacy* boundary. On the Internet, someone can cross a privacy boundary no matter where they are.

A Little Bit More About Privacy

Privacy can mean a lot of things, but simply put, it is when you are being left alone, free from the attention of others.
Online privacy is a major issue. If you use a social media site like Facebook, you may think that what you write or post is only able to be seen by your "friends" or "followers," but this isn't always true. The Internet is a complicated place, and you can't assume that anything you post will stay private. If you use social media networks, learn more about their privacy settings and how to use them properly.

One time I saw a picture on my big sister's social media account. It was of a friend of hers from school. People were teasing the girl in the comments. My sister was upset and said everyone was "sharing it." Were those kids crossing a boundary?

Yes, they definitely were. And you know what? They crossed your sister's boundaries too, because seeing that mean post was not her choice, and she was probably feeling sad and angry that those people were violating her friend's privacy and boundaries. It's never okay to post pictures of someone else online without their permission, and it's also wrong to bully people, whether in real life or online.

Online Bullying

Online bullying is also called *cyberbullying*. It's harassment that takes place through social media platforms such as Facebook, Snapchat, Instagram and Twitter, or through texting, emailing, online messaging, web forums, video games and so on. The bully posts negative, hurtful and harmful content about another person or group of people. The purpose is usually to embarrass and hurt the person or group by sharing private and personal information about them.

Unlike bullying at school, cyberbullying can go on 24 hours a day, whenever kids are accessing their computers, tablets or smartphones. And this type of bullying can be anonymous, meaning that sometimes you can't even tell who the bully is because they are using a made-up name. People who are cyberbullied often feel intensely alone, isolated and afraid.

If someone posts something inappropriate or mean on the Internet, can they erase it or say they are sorry?

Yes, sometimes. But the problem is, other people have already seen it, so it never really goes away. People can use their phones or computers to save a picture before the person who made the post erases it. It is best never to post anything on the Internet that is rude, personal or crosses a boundary, because once it is online, it's there for everyone to see, and you can't really take it back.

If you have private thoughts or feelings that you want to let out, you can talk to a trusted adult, or write or draw about what you are feeling in a journal that is just for you.

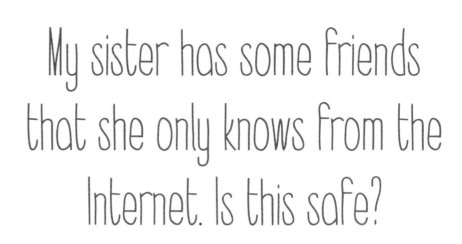

My sister has some friends that she only knows from the Internet. Is this safe?

Online Friends vs. Real-Life Friends

- **Online Friends**: These are friends you know only through online networking platforms such as Facebook, Twitter, Instagram and Snapchat, or through online forums/chat rooms and gaming sites. They are friends you will rarely, if ever, meet.
- **Real-Life Friends**: These are friends you know and see in real life. They're people with whom you share feelings of affection and respect and similar values or interests.

That's a good question. Some people do use the internet and social media to make new friends. It's important to be cautious of people you meet on the internet, though, because it is hard to know for sure if they are telling the truth about who they are, where they live and why they want to get to know you. Always ask an adult first before you communicate online with anybody you don't know in real life. Your parents can help you decide if it is okay and what information is appropriate to share.

What should I do if something or someone on the Internet makes me feel uncomfortable?

You should always tell your parents or teacher right away. Never feel embarrassed or bad that you saw something you didn't like. It is not your fault that other people cross boundaries online.

Thinking about this stuff makes me
kind of uncomfortable and angry.
I don't like to feel this way.

I understand how you feel. It's normal to feel sad or worried when we learn about some of the bad things that can happen in the world. However, it's important to know that we don't have to accept it. We can practice using our own good judgment and respecting boundaries, and we can encourage each other to be respectful of boundaries and use good judgment too.

Do people ever use the Internet for good things?

Yes, they sure do! A lot of people, from all parts of the world, use the Internet to do awesome things, like educate people who can't go to school, raise money to help people who are in need and bring positive change to their communities.

Crowdfunding for Good

Crowdfunding is raising money and public attention from a large group of people, including friends, family members, the general public, companies, investors and so on. Crowdfunding is usually done online through social media or specific crowdfunding sites such as GoFundMe.com. People can pledge money to a certain cause, project, product or organization.

Meet Braeden Quinn

Braeden was passionate about ending food insecurity for families and children, so he took action. He created his own nonprofit called 3B Brae's Brown Bags to help those in need fight against hunger. With the money he has raised through crowdfunding, Braeden has put together bags with water, fruit and other snacks for those in need in his local community. He has delivered more than 1,200 bags to shelters and soup kitchens in his community.

What about me? How can I use the Internet in a way that will be good for me and others?

There are many things you can do! When your parents say it's okay to start using social media, you can decide to post only things that are respectful and kind. Or you can ask your parents to show you a story about someone who is working to make the world a better place and ask them to "share" or "like" it. You can also model good boundaries for your friends and the adults in your life by behaving in a way that is respectful to others and yourself.

Meet Malala Yousafzai

Malala is an online role model. She is a person who serves as a good example by influencing others. When she was a young woman, she was badly hurt by a group of people she had spoken out against because they didn't believe in educating girls. Malala survived and has become a well-known activist for education and women's rights in the Middle East and all over the globe. She uses social media as a force for good, advocating for the causes she believes in to over a million Twitter followers.

The adults in your life can also help you develop an online safety plan. Here are some tips to help you use the Internet safely.

Social Media Guidelines for Staying Safe Online

- Don't post pictures or content about other people (like friends) without their permission, even if your intentions are good. Always ask if it is okay to share a picture or reference someone else in your post.

- Don't talk to people online who you have never met before (unless you have checked with your parents).

- Ask your parents before creating an account on a new social media platform.

- Use the privacy settings for all social media accounts to make sure your personal information and content are private.

- Accept as friends on social media only people who are also friends in real life.

- If you come across something online that makes you uncomfortable, tell your parents or a teacher right away.

- Never share your passwords or log-in information with anyone except your parents.

- Have your parents or teacher help you turn off your location services on all social media platforms.

- Don't spend your whole day online. Become aware of how much time you are spending on your phone or computer. If your parents haven't set a limit for how long you can be on your devices each day, set one yourself.

- **THINK** before you post:

  T: is it True?
  H: is it Helpful?
  I: is it Inspiring?
  N: is it Necessary?
  K: is it Kind?

When each of us sets and respects smart boundaries, and when we help others understand them, we can make the Internet, and the world around us, a more respectful and positive place.

Note from Dr. Jillian Roberts, Author and Child Psychologist

I have noticed through my work that kids who use the Internet and interact on the Web are struggling to understand online boundaries, and their parents, who did not grow up with this kind of technology, do not always know how to help. As technological development accelerates, we have access to information and people in an unprecedented way. As a child psychologist, I think it's important for experts to provide parents and kids with concrete tools and resources they can use to engage in conversations about the changing world. This is why I first developed my app, started to write these books and co-founded FamilySparks. I believe that by starting these conversations with children when they are young, and engaging them and listening to them, we, as the grown-ups in their lives whom they love and trust, can help them navigate these difficult waters and learn to be positive online role models.

References

3B Brae's Brown Bag Foundation: braesbrownbags.org

Fundable: What is Crowdfunding?: fundable.com/learn/resources/guides/
crowdfunding-guide/what-is-crowdfunding

Malala Fund: malala.org

THINK Acronym—The Coaching Tools Company: thecoachingtoolscompany.com

Resources

Websites for Children:

Canadian Centre for Child Protection—Zoe & Molly Online: zoeandmolly.ca

Canadian Centre for Child Protection—Need Help Now: needhelpnow.ca

Canada's Centre for Digital and Media Literacy—Media Smarts educational games:
mediasmarts.ca/digital-media-literacy/educational-games

Justice Education Society—Cybersafe BC: cybersafebc.ca

Websites for Parents:

Canadian Centre for Child Protection—Need Help Now: needhelpnow.ca

Cyber Bully Help: Preventing Bullying in the Digital Age: cyberbullyhelp.com

Family Online Safety Institute—Good Digital Parenting: fosi.org/good-digital-parenting

FamilySparks—Resources for parents, teachers and others who support children:
familysparks.com

Government of Canada's Get Cyber Safe—getcybersafe.gc.ca/index-eng.aspx

Protect Kids Online: protectkidsonline.ca

Dr. Jillian Roberts is a renowned child psychologist, author, professor and parent. Considered a go-to child psychology expert for journalists, Dr. Roberts has had her work published in the *New York Times* and the *Toronto Sun*, and is a regular contributor to *HuffPost*, Global News and CBC. She is the author of two bestselling and award-winning series of children's books: the Just Enough series explains topics like birth and diversity to children ages 3–6, while The World Around Us series introduces kids ages 5–8 to issues like poverty and online safety. She lives in Victoria, British Columbia.

Jane Heinrichs is a children's book writer and illustrator. She is the author/illustrator of the hybrid graphic novel *Every Home Needs An Elephant*. She starts her day at a clear desk with her huge sketchbook (for books) and her tiny sketchbook (for daily drawings) but usually ends up sitting on the floor, surrounded by a collection of paints, pencils and papers. Jane lives in the United Kingdom with her family.

THE WORLD AROUND US series

These inquiry-based books are an excellent cross-curricular resource encouraging children to explore and discuss important issues and **foster their own compassion and empathy.**

AGES 6–8 · 32 PAGES FULL-COLOR PHOTOGRAPHS · RESOURCES INCLUDED

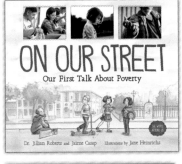

ON OUR STREET
Our First Talk About Poverty
Dr. Jillian Roberts and Jaime Casap   Illustrations by Jane Heinrichs

ON THE NEWS
Our First Talk About Tragedy
Dr. Jillian Roberts   Illustrations by Jane Heinrichs

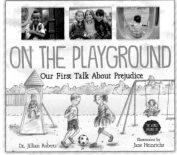

ON THE PLAYGROUND
Our First Talk About Prejudice
Dr. Jillian Roberts   Illustrations by Jane Heinrichs

UNDER OUR CLOTHES
Our First Talk About Our Bodies
Dr. Jillian Roberts   Illustrations by Jane Heinrichs

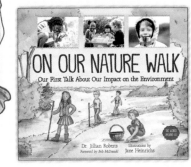

ON OUR NATURE WALK
Our First Talk About Our Impact on the Environment
Dr. Jillian Roberts   Illustrations by Jane Heinrichs

THE WORLD AROUND US

TheWorldAroundUsSeries.com